Bag
Green
Guilt

Bag

Green

Guilt

Five Easy Steps:
Turn Eco-Anxiety Into
Constructive Energy

By Jen Pleasants

Published by
Show The Love Media LLC
www.showthelove.com

Edited by
Deborah Roth

Cover Design by
Deborah Roth and George Ivanel

Text Setting by
George Ivanel

The mission of Show The Love Media is to publish content that is inspirational, entertaining and beneficial to humankind.

A percentage of the revenues from the sale of this book go to environmental charities. Show The Love Media is a member of One Percent for the Planet.

Please recycle this book when you are finished reading, or pass it on to a friend or library. If you are reading an electronic version of this book: even better!

Printed in the United States by LSI

Dedications

Dedicated to my children - Jack, James and Josie for their patience with me while I try to make it all better.

Acknowledgements

Thank you Mom and Dad for your endless love and support.

Oh, and I couldn't have done any of this without my stellar editor, Deborah Roth, who makes me sound much more together than I actually am!

And, lastly to my True Love, ILMSF.

Table of Contents

GETTING STARTED

"Change has a considerable psychological impact on the human mind. To the fearful it is threatening because it means that things may get worse. To the hopeful it is encouraging because things may get better. To the confident it is inspiring because the challenge exists to make things better."
-King Whitney Jr.

change yourself, change the world

I started writing this book with the goal of easing the pressure we feel to be eco-green-Earth-saving-superheroes. I wanted to inspire readers to transform their feelings of guilt and anxiety into power and action and for them to really believe that their actions can change the world.

So I did a lot of research, most of which, surprisingly, suggested that individual recycling efforts *don't* make a dent in the critical issue of global warming and the environment. To make any kind of significant impact would take immediate, 100% compliant action on the parts of governments, corporations, people and countries.

After that I became depressed wondering if my buying recycled toilet paper and organic cotton shirts really accomplished anything at all. I thought *why bother?*

Then I read this quote:

"When I was a young man, I wanted to change the world. I found it was difficult to change the world, so I tried to change my nation.

When I found I couldn't change my nation, I began to focus on my town.

I couldn't change the town and as an older man, I tried to change my family.

Now, as an old man, I realize the only thing I can change is myself, and suddenly I realize that if long ago I had changed myself, I could have made an impact on my family. My family and I could have made an impact on our town.

*Their impact could have changed the nation and **I could indeed have changed the world.**"*

-I Wanted To Change The World
Unknown Monk

So, what I do DOES matter. What you do does too.

Individually and together we *can* make the difference needed to return the Earth to a healthier and better place for us, our children and their children.

That's a lot of responsibility, and as any mother knows: with great responsibility, comes great guilt.

This book was created to get rid of green guilt, eradicate eco-anxiety and *make it all better.* (That's my personal motto, the motto of my company, and really, the motto of any mom!)

Why *Green* Guilt?
The marketplace is saturated with *green* books.

Green was the most overused word last year.

Green is SO yesterday.

In today's world there is *so much* pressure to be green. The by-products are 'eco-anxiety' and 'green guilt.'

We need to learn how to funnel those feelings into constructive channels, and feel reassured that what we do *does* make a difference.

For the rest of the book, when I refer to 'green guilt' I am referring to the combined feeling of guilt and anxiety that we feel in regards to the environment, but in truth they are different things.

One is actual guilt: when you feel bad because sometimes you knowingly don't do the 'right' green thing. This is different than eco-anxiety, which is when you feel overwhelmed and helpless because everything you and the rest of the world are doing feels as though it is having some kind of bad eco-repercussion. I want to eradicate these toxic emotions so that we are free to use that energy to lift us up rather than drag us down.

My Plan

Hi. I am Jen, and I have green guilt.

This is a five-step program that I've created to help myself and anyone else who suffers from these feelings.

And if you answer *yes* or even *sometimes* to any of the following questions then this book should help you feel better.

- Do you feel bad that you are not driving a hybrid?

- Have you stopped fully enjoying taking long hot showers because you know they waste water and energy?

- Do you feel at fault when you forget to bring your own bags to the grocery store?

- Do you feel helpless when you hear that the glaciers are melting, the sea levels are rising, and that polar bears are disappearing?

You Are Not Alone
A survey by *USA Today* showed that in 2008 22% of people, primarily women, felt some kind of green guilt.

And it isn't a new feeling for most of us… I just looked and it was in April 2007 that I registered the website NoGreenGuilt.com. I wanted a whole site dedicated to this topic but it evolved instead into my current site, showtheLOVE.com, a site that combines eco things with fashion and celebrity to make it more fun.

In Northern California, where I live, if you don't already feel bad about not being green enough someone: a friend, an associate, or a complete stranger, will make sure you do!

Take the car thing. I have three kids and I drive a minivan. Many others around me drive some kind of hybrid. I know that hybrids are better for reducing CO_2 emissions but I can't fit three kids in a Prius or even a Highlander comfortably. I remind myself of this interesting fact: a raw vegan foodist driving a Hummer leaves a *smaller* carbon footprint than a meat eating Prius driver. (It's true! More on the why and how in Chapter 3.)

I still have hybrid envy.

My neighbor Kathy told me recently about an episode she had: she said that when she reached for a paper towel in her kitchen she knew she should instead just use the dishtowel to dry her hands but then she wondered... does the energy and water it takes to wash the dishtowel make it wiser to use the paper towel? Which is worse? Turns out, the paper towel is, in fact, paper towels are responsible for 3,000 tons of waste...*daily*. Then Kathy said she looked at her kids watching TV on the carpeted floor and started to have a meltdown – the synthetic carpet was probably off-gassing toxic fumes, yikes! – it is all so overwhelming!

Problem of Riches

Green guilt sometimes is seen as a high-class problem. If, like billions of people on this Earth, you don't have electricity, don't drive a car or don't have enough food to eat, then worrying about things like switching to CFL light bulbs, exhaust pollution, or buying organic food might not seem like issues at all. In fact, most people in the world aren't agonizing over things like that; instead, they are agonizing over REAL problems like providing food, shelter and clothing for their families. (Even if you are feeling the pinch of the global recession - and who isn't at this point? - if you are reading this book then you probably have change in your pocket and are not in as bad of a way as more than half the people on this planet.)

Green guilt might only be felt by some, but global warming is being felt (or soon will be felt) by everyone whether they realize it or not. *You* probably realize it, which is why you're reading this book! Global warming is affecting the world's poorest the most. Food production, water supplies, public health, and livelihoods are all being damaged and undermined due to climate change. Of course, this makes me feel more resolved to do my part with my "embarrassment of riches" to reduce the impact of consumption on the environment overall.

YOU CAN TOO.

"Out beyond the idea of wrong doing and right doing, there is a field. I'll meet you there."
-Rumi

We are learning new things every day about what is helpful or harmful to ourselves and the environment. What was once safe is now toxic, what was once the best way to do something is now the worst way to do something. Just peeking back at our childhood reveals how much of what we learned growing up has changed.

And who even knows if what we think *now* is really right?! About a year ago my brother horrified me and, as a result, shifted my paradigm. He told me that by walking to my local restaurant, only one mile down the road, I actually had a bigger carbon footprint than if I drove. He said that I burned more calories walking there, became hungrier, and ate extra food that I wouldn't normally have eaten, and that the carbon footprint of the processes used to get that food to me outweighed the impact of the gas I would have used in my car to drive to the restaurant!

So no one *really* knows what is wholly right or wrong but the important thing is to not to feel bad about our actions if we have good intentions and are doing the things we are capable of to move ourselves, our families, and our communities forward to a better world. It is a waste of our OWN energy to feel guilty or have anxiety about what we should be doing when we could use that same energy constructively.

Mind Blowing Change

Another reason to be gentle on ourselves is that there have been so many paradigm shifts in the last ten years. I will forever remember what I was doing when I heard that planes had crashed into New York's World Trade Center, and on a different but also disturbing note, how I felt when I first watched Al Gore's film: *An Inconvenient Truth.*

Thanks to our vast and sophisticated media we now live in a true Global Village where we have the ability to hear of events almost instantaneously, regardless of location. Increased global knowledge leads to an increased sense of global responsibility. And we have risen to that responsibility: think of how many people you know that were able to rapidly learn of and donate to various organizations when the tsunami hit eleven countries around the Indian Ocean in 2004 or the earthquake in China in 2008.

Those were dramatic and traumatic events. And as we all know, but tend to forget, there are still AIDS orphans in sub-Saharan Africa, victims of war in Gaza, Darfur refugees, and underprivileged kids right here in my own neighborhood, and probably yours as well. And the list the goes on.

My email inbox is overflowing with people sending yet another online petition to save the wolves, ocean, children or rainforests etc., and if I simply delete those pleas for help I feel like a bad person. Most people I know are stressed to the max just trying to sort out their own lives let alone anyone else's.

It is hard to get hit with all of this information and not want to crawl in a hole and hide.

"Successful guilt is the bane of society."
- Publilius Syrus

It is Hard to Change, but It is Our Responsibility
We shouldn't feel bad for not being able to quickly morph into Mr. or Ms. Green Jeans and save our ailing planet. **But we should, as conscientious keepers of the keys to the future, start taking daily steps to change the impact of our past.**

As we learn new things it becomes even more challenging to adapt and break old behavioral patterns that have been years in the making. However, beating ourselves up when we fail to be perfectly 'green,' is not the answer. Ignoring the guilt isn't the answer either (you already know that, that's why you're holding this book right now!)

There is an easy way to funnel eco-anxiety and green guilt into the right channels. And I am hoping by the time you finish *Bag Green Guilt* that you will stop feeling helpless and start feeling more goal oriented and self-fulfilled in working toward our common focus of gluing this planet back together.

What to Do?!
There are many books that will tell you what you SHOULD be doing (about everything, not just about being green). I wrote *this* book to share the emotions of what we are all feeling around the topic of the environment as well as help us be and feel more

powerful.

So, don't feel bad for not doing everything. However, if you WERE feeling bad about not doing *anything*... perhaps you know deep down in your heart that we all must band together and change our habits or the whole world will go to pot?

"It is not work that kills men, it is worry. Work is healthy; you can hardly put more on a man than he can bear. But worry is rust upon the blade. It is not movement that destroys the machinery, but friction."
-Henry Ward Beecher

So I came up with a five-step program that helped me refocus and regain control by switching out toxic paralyzing emotions for healthy empowering ones. I hope it helps you too and there is only one way to find out...

THE FIVE-STEP PROGRAM TO BAG GREEN GUILT

1. breathe
   take a BIG deep breath, now exhale!

2. acknowledge
   that you can't do *everything*;
   affirm
   that you can do *something*.

3. write
   down all (or just some) of the things that make you feel
   eco-anxious or guilty.

4. act
   pick *one* thing to do that is 'green' that you aren't already
   doing and start doing that one thing this week. Do that
   one thing WELL. You'll feel better doing one thing well
   than eight things poorly.

5. praise
   make a mental note to say something positive to yourself,
   your family, your friends, your community, your compa-
   ny or your country whenever a step is taken in the right
   direction.

Let's Get Started!

STEP 1

"Sometimes the most important thing in a whole day is the rest
we take between two deep breaths."
-Etty Hillesum

breathe

Take a BIG deep breath. Now exhale!

Okay, it turns out that it is actually a really important thing to
breathe. And I mean breathe *right*. If you do, it will change your
life as it physically and mentally affects you for the better. No
great insight there, we all know that, but few of us take the time
to do it right!

My mentor on breathing (and life) is an amazing human named
Sri Sri Ravi Shankar. He is a world spiritual leader and Nobel
Peace Prize nominee who, among other things, founded the Art
of Living (www.artofliving.org) and created a series of breathing
techniques which, when done regularly, enhance our physical,
spiritual and emotional well being. Sri Sri emphasizes the link
between the body and mind. He says, "Breath holds the secret to

our mind, to our inner life, and there are patterns in our breath that link us to the universe."

His organization, the ArtOfLiving.org, is in more than 140 different countries and offers courses all over the world on breathing and meditation. I took a class and was transformed. I needed less sleep when I took the time to do the breathing exercises every day, and my memory was so sharp! I normally have a rotten memory, but during the course, and for about a week after, I was crystal clear. Oh, and did I mention it helps your skin, so you look younger? I saw two women I know, in their late forties, take ten years off their faces by doing the daily breathing exercises.

There have been several independent studies on the numerous mental and physical health benefits of the course. The studies have been published in international peer-reviewed journals and confirm what participants of the course find out firsthand: breathing right makes a huge difference in your quality of life.

Eventually, I talked my husband into taking the course, and he SO doesn't go that way, but he did it for me (he's dreamy like that). And guess what? He benefited from it so much that he took the second course, which even I haven't taken! Anyway, I'm digressing. The point is, breathing helps make you feel all better and can rid you of guilt! Sri Sri writes:

"Much of the stress or limitations in life come from vacillating between regret about the past or worry about the future. And yet, the present is the only place that happiness can be experienced."

"No breath, no life, know breath KNOW life!"
-Sri Sri Ravi Shankar

Western doctors agree with my Eastern Guru. According to Dr.

Diana Walcutt, psychologist and anxiety specialist:

"Ninety percent of the people we ask don't breathe in a way that can help them master their stress. It truly is something that you have to learn and practice, practice, practice for over two weeks before you can get it right."

Dr. Andrew Weil concurs: "Practicing regular, mindful breathing can be calming and energizing and can even help with stress-related health problems ranging from panic attacks to digestive disorders."

Breathing is a powerful tool in coping with and overcoming stress and guilt. I better breathe mindfully right now... deep breath... Ahhhhhhhhhh!

Oh, one more thought on this - it is a GREAT thing to teach your children. They have stress too, and few tools to get rid of it (well, which we approve of: hitting your sister doesn't count!) Breathing and meditation are not just for adults. Teaching kids this stuff early on is a great gift. I had my son Jack take an Art of Living kid's class (Art Excel), when he was just eight and he is so much easier to live with now ☺.

*"**Breathe**. Let go. And remind yourself that this very moment is the only one you know you have for sure."*
-Oprah Winfrey

What does breathing right have to do with saving the environment?

Everything.

I firmly believe that you can only focus on doing the 'extras' when you're feeling less stressed. We're all stressed to the max and accepting additional responsibility for being green

IS stressful. As you know, NOT accepting responsibility for being green is ALSO stressful. So breathe. Breathe when you're driving, sitting at your desk or anytime you feel anxiety coming on!

Breathe. I promise you: it will make it all better.

So, step number one involves doing just one of the following (but you should feel free to do more than one if you have the time and energy):

- Set aside 20 minutes a day (okay, even five will do) to be by yourself and do some deep breathing. (For specific exercises visit www.showthelove. com/breathe).
- If you can't get time to yourself to practice breathing have your kids join you as they need a tool to de-stress as well.
- Check out www.artofliving.org and sign up for a local class to learn breathing techniques that have been proven to work. I bet it will change your life!

STEP 2

Now that you are *breathing* properly you should feel more energized, more clearheaded, and have less of stress pit in your gut. But we are just beginning to rid ourselves of this gnawing green guilt. Let's move on to the next step.

Acknowledge that you can't do *everything*;
Affirm that you can do *something*.

You know it is true but remind yourself, seriously, that you can't do everything, but you can do *some* things, and that's good enough. Acknowledge! (And don't forget to breathe.) These environmental issues have been decades in the making and it will take years and the efforts of millions of people to fix them, so take it easy on yourself. At the same time, make sure that you are one of those millions making an effort because that is how we are going to be able to extend the life of the planet for our children.

Psychologist Lynn O'Connor, a professor who specializes in guilt at the Wright Institute in Berkley, California was quoted in *USA Today* as saying, "That sort of "omnipotent" guilt - when people have an exaggerated sense of their own power - is quite common. You really are not responsible for the whole planet nearing extinction."

So many of us get overwhelmed by all of the things that need to get done to fix our sick Earth that we become paralyzed and shove our heads in the sand only to become more stressed out.

In any case, just pausing for a moment to acknowledge that this responsibility does not lie on your shoulders alone but on all of our shoulders together is a necessary step in not feeling too overwhelmed.

After we *acknowledge* that we can't do everything we must also *affirm* that we can and will do something.

Realizing that you can't do it all should not be a cop-out to do nothing but instead a release from the feeling of having to do everything.

Okay – so how do we affirm? Through *Affirmations*.

Affirmations are a powerful tool to use for all parts of your life. According to DailyPositiveAffirmation.com:

"Positive affirmations lead your subconscious mind into believing the opposite of the negative thoughts that pervade your mind. It is just like brainwashing only this time, you can choose which perception to change. The words you say to boost your performance and thoughts are positive affirmations. By using words of encouragement to modify your views on action or inaction, you are able to instill in your subconscious mind the necessary positive changes that you need to overcome fear of failure. And by barraging your subconscious mind into believing that you can do it you are slowly washing away that old negative mindset and paving the way for a new outlook.

Affirmations can come in the form of positive statements, usually short, that aim to challenge the negative beliefs you have about yourself or your abilities. These daily affirmations are meant to replace the negative beliefs that undermine your belief in yourself."

TheMentalFitnessCenter.com agrees, posting that "It's impossible to entertain a negative thought if you're honed in on a positive one, which is why it's even more important to fill your mind with plenty of positive thoughts, or affirmations."

I don't know about you, but my thoughts are often in pictures, so I find visualization to be a huge help when practicing affirmations. Don't just say it, think it, and picture it.

I started using visualization about twenty years ago after reading the best-seller, *Creative Visualization* by Shakti Gawain, and I attribute so many of my blessings today to using these techniques. Gawain was way ahead of her time, publishing her work decades before modern visualization books like *The Secret* became popular.

Gawain has so many key insights in her book, but as far as visualization, she recommends four basic steps:

1. Create a clear idea or picture.
2. Focus on it often.
3. Give it positive energy.
4. Set your goal.

So what would an affirmation and visualization look like that would rid you of green guilt? You can make up any you like that feel right to you, but here are some I like to use:

- **I am part of the solution** – visualize world leaders (or your children) thanking you for your contribution to a healthy Earth.

- **We are solving global warming** – what would a truly green and healthy planet look like?

- **I have an abundance of energy** – imagine yourself jumping for joy.

- **I radiate love and happiness** – think of an aura of beautiful colors emanating from you.

- **I am powerful** – picture feeling strong enough physically and mentally to handle anything that comes your way.

- **I am making a difference** – imagine a single green act you do and the planet saying thank you.

- **I am embracing the green and eco-lifestyle** – look in the mirror at yourself reading this book!

- **I am healthy and happy** – imagine yourself on a mountain-top surrounded by wildflowers where you are taking a deep breath and celebrating your strong healthy body.

- **I am safe and everything is working out for the higher good** – visualize being wrapped in a huge comfy blanket in a truly safe place.

- **I am receiving infinite energy from the universe** – think of the sun giving life sustaining energy to the world.

- **Every little bit does make a difference** - imagine each person doing their part for a perfectly harmonious planet.

When doing affirmations remember that to get the most benefit they must be in the present tense. Picture yourself now, not 10 years from now. It is important to get rid of negative terms in your affirmations like "not," "no," "can't," "won't," and others. They also must be brief, easily repeatable and easily pictured as repeating them and visualizing them over and over again with genuine positive emotion is the key.

Another kind of affirmation I like uses the power of gratitude. "I am grateful for the air I breathe," or "I am grateful for this beautiful day and the sun, sky and trees" or whatever the case might be. Not only does being grateful help you feel happier and more at peace but it opens you up to receive an abundance of blessings.

I was reassured of this message when I was late one day for an Art of Living Meditation class. I ran into class after having "the worst morning". I can't remember now all of the things that went wrong, but it was pouring down rain, I had been up all night with the baby, I got lost trying to get there, etc. I continued to explain all of the rotten things that had happened on my way to class, then I stopped and said, but all of that aside, I am so blessed, none of those are real problems, I am really so lucky to be here. The teacher was proud to see I had come to this realization and told me that Sri Sri (my Guru I mentioned earlier) often quotes Jesus and says **"Those who Have will be Given More, Those Who Have Little Will Be Given Less."**

If you see your glass as half full and are grateful for even the little that you might have then more blessings will come your way and vice versa! As this relates to the environment, I try not to look at only the bad things that are happening to the Earth, but I try to be grateful for its wonders and beauty. According to BeliefNet. com:

"Psychologists Robert Emmons of U.C. Davis and Michael McCullough of the University of Miami have found that practicing gratitude can actually improve our emotional and physical wellbeing. Their ongoing Research Project on Gratitude and Thankfulness has found that people who keep weekly gratitude journals had fewer physical symptoms, exercised more, had a better outlook on life and were more likely to reach their goals."

I personally believe that if we all shifted our mindset to a more grateful one, a lot of the world's problems would disappear, but don't get me started on that now!

To complete step number two in this Five-Step Program, do the following:

- **Think of and write down your own empowering affirmations and visualizations.**
- **Repeat the affirmations and visualizations with passion throughout your day. An especially good time would be right after you do breathing exercises but any time of day is good too.**

STEP 3

"The greatest of faults, I should say, is to be conscious of none."
-Thomas Carlyle

So you are now *breathing* properly, you have *acknowledged* that you can't do everything, and you have *affirmed* that you can do something. Now in order to determine what else you can do to lessen your guilt and anxiety, we have to figure out what specifically is causing stress in the first place.

Therefore, in this chapter, we are going to make a huge list of things that are on our minds. Brace yourself, because my list is a little (okay, a lot) out of control. At some points you might feel like you are getting more stressed out by reading what is bothering me, but I promise this is a part of the process, so stick with it, and you will feel better in the end.

And so we begin the next step. (You might want to take a few breaths before delving into this one.)

<u>write</u>

Write down all (or as many as you can) of the things that make you feel eco-anxious and guilty.

I am a big fan of writing down everything that overwhelms you (just writing this book helped me a ton!) You can either keep to just green things or write your entire life down depending on how much time and paper you have ☺. On second thought, this is a book about feeling less green guilt, so just write down the eco-stuff. Or type it out on your computer screen! When you are done circle your top three stressors.

Some things that are on my list:

- Taking long showers
- Ordering endangered fish at a restaurant
- Buying clothes made of non-organic fabric
- Driving a gas guzzler
- Throwing away uneaten food
- Not lobbying Congress for clean energy
- Keeping the house extra warm in the winter
- Using paper towels
- Using plastic bags
- All of the junk mail I receive
- Forgetting to bring my own bags to the grocery
- Not buying organic food for my kids
- Not carpooling
- Throwing away broken electronics
- Tossing batteries in the trash
- Owning ten pairs of jeans

In case you don't feel like writing your list down you can share mine, I promise, it is big enough for all of us!

However... my list is not limited to the above. Over the next bit of this book I am going to break down into categories the things that cause me green guilt and go into my resolution on each. Remember – our goal isn't to be perfect. It is just to make a difference.

At times you might feel overwhelmed reading all of this information but remember: it is not easy to shift our mindsets but education is a necessary step in the process of healing ourselves and the Earth.

In fact, I encourage you NOT to read the next section all at once. Pick it up, put it down, keep it in your purse or pocket to glance at when you're waiting somewhere.

And remember that the unloading of green guilt is meant to be cathartic. And even if we don't have time to deal with our feelings at least they are now out in the open and not buried deeply and festering away in our emotional and environmentally toxic landfills.

Take a breath – and here we go!

My Green Guilt (by category):

Food and Drink

Most everyone feels guilty about food: when we eat, how much we eat, where we eat, what we eat, and how we eat. Food can be downright nauseating!

"Providing food is the single largest human activity on the planet, occupying over 40% of the planet's bio-capacity...this activity is diminishing the Earth's capacity to regenerate itself and sustain us."
- Andrew Kang Bartlett, author of *Energy Food and You.*

Let's start with a big one... *organic food.* I have major guilt when I choose non-organic over organic food for my children as I know I should feed them as well as possible. Thankfully, I am learning that I can safely get away with not buying ALL things organic. But there are some items that are non-negotiable for me because the non-organic versions are laden with pesticides.

Following is a *very* helpful list of 43 fruits and vegetables that contain the highest level of pesticides. If I only buy a few organic items they will be the foods at the top of this list!

From one of my favorite organizations the Environmental Working Group (EWG)

The Full List: 43 Fruits & Veggies

RANK	FRUIT OR VEGGIE	SCORE
1 (worst)	Peaches	100 (highest pesticide load)
2	Apples	96
3	Sweet Bell Peppers	86
4	Celery	85
5	Nectarines	84
6	Strawberries	83
7	Cherries	75
8	Lettuce	69
9	Grapes - Imported	68
10	Pears	65
11	Spinach	60
12	Potatoes	58
13	Carrots	57
14	Green Beans	55
15	Hot Peppers	53
16	Cucumbers	52
17	Raspberries	47
18	Plums	46
19	Oranges	46
20	Grapes-Domestic	46
21	Cauliflower	39
22	Tangerine	38
23	Mushrooms	37
24	Cantaloupe	34
25	Lemon	31
26	Honeydew Melon	31
27	Grapefruit	31
28	Winter Squash	31
29	Tomatoes	30
30	Sweet Potatoes	30
31	Watermelon	25
32	Blueberries	24
33	Papaya	21
34	Eggplant	19
35	Broccoli	18
36	Cabbage	17
37	Bananas	16
38	Kiwi	14
39	Asparagus	11
40	Sweet Peas-Frozen	11
41	Mango	9
42	Pineapples	7
43	Sweet Corn-Frozen	2
44	Avocado	1
45 (best)	Onions	1 (lowest pesticide load)

There are people who say that locally grown produce is more important than organically grown or that you should only eat 'in season' produce (which for me means no lettuce in the winter, which is not going to happen). Recently, I found out that all of this debate is in vain.

Here's why:

Kristin Underwood, who writes about eco-friendly farming at treehugger.com, reports that while we are worrying about what is best, organic vs. local, the truth is it doesn't matter. NEITHER IS SUSTAINABLE. Kristin writes on TreeHugger.com:

"While last year we were debating whether it's better to buy organic or local (or both), an article in *Mother Jones* now reports that we have even bigger fish to fry when it comes to our food production. While dreams of our future food system may rely on the romantic image of local farmers, the reality is: this model can't do what we need it to do, that is, feed billions of people.

Future food must also pack a greater amount of calories using fewer resources (water and energy), as well as be affordable, "ecologically benign" and also not abuse laborers and farmers in the process. Most of what we consider "sustainable" today is not - according to the article, only 2% of the food purchased in the US qualifies as sustainable (i.e. adheres to the values listed above). Growing food organically but underpaying workers, or using small-scale local farms really only gets at one part of the equation and won't work to feed the billions of people on the planet long-term.

In that case, is it better to purchase your food from a farmers market, where dozens of farmers truck in their produce each on individual trucks from all over, or purchase your food from a chain store where they ship it en masse, via large trucks? Considering the transport only accounts for 10% of the emissions from food production, maybe we should turn our focus over to how the food is produced (resource usage)."

It is a wonderful thing that people are finally focusing on these issues. I love that the movie *Food, Inc.* exposes the current food industry's dark secrets and addresses our nation's (and world's) need for healthier, more nutrient-dense food. If you have not yet seen it, check it out!

A recent report from Carnegie-Mellon University said, "going meat and dairyless one day a week is more environmentally beneficial than eating locally every single day." *(source: Mother Jones, Spoiled: Organic and Local is So 2008, April 2009)*

Remember the paradigm shift my brother set in motion in the story I related at the beginning of the book? We would make a larger impact on reducing carbon emissions by being a vegan than by driving a hybrid, and you will see why – in greater detail – in a minute and it is fascinating. I am not a vegan (though I aspire to be), but my friends Share and Bam are and they have the coolest site and cooking shows at RawPirateGourmet.com. If you are looking for a weight-loss plan or just a feel-good or save-the-world-plan that raw vegan thing is a silver bullet. But I know for most people (even me) going 100% raw is WAY too crunchy and over the top – even 50% is admirable! I was just throwing that out there just in case you were looking for a bandwagon to jump on! For more details check out raw food books by author, Natalia Rose or the website of raw food chef, Diana Stobo: dianastobo. com.

On the meatless topic, one thing you should know is that the number one reason for deforestation of the rainforests is *cows* (i.e. Americans' need for hamburgers - it's not the cows' fault). Those burgers/steaks are something we can all leave off our tables, which will make us healthier, probably thinner and the world better off overall.

From *The New York Times* article '*Rethinking the Meat Guzzler*,' January 27, 2008, "Growing meat (it's hard to use the word "raising" when applied to animals in factory farms) uses so many resources that it's a challenge to enumerate them all. But consider: an estimated 30 percent of the Earth's ice-free land is directly or indirectly involved in livestock production."

Here are the top four reasons I removed beef from my diet:

Water
EarthSave.org reports that, "It takes 2,500 gallons of water to produce one pound of beef. This could be used to grow more than 50 pounds of fruits and vegetables. Half of all water consumed in the United States is used to grow feed and provide drinking water for cattle and other livestock."

The Wall Street Journal notes: "A typical hamburger [1/4 pound] takes 630 gallons of water to produce – more than three times the amount the average American uses every day for drinking, bathing, washing dishes and flushing toilets."

Grain
It takes almost 11 pounds of grain to produce one pound of hamburger. (source WorldWatch.org) This could make 8 loaves of bread or 24 plates of spaghetti. Grain consumption by livestock is increasing twice as fast as grain consumption by people. Cattle consume more than half all U.S. grain. (source EarthSave.org)

Methane
Methane is a gas that is produced by bacteria in the digestive tracks of animals. Of all the methane gas released by animals, a whopping 75% comes from cows!

Nearly a fifth of the world's greenhouse gases are generated by livestock production – that's more greenhouse gases than are produced by vehicles. (source: The United Nation's Food and Agriculture Organization)

Methane is 20 times more potent than carbon dioxide and could be more problematic than CO_2 for global warming. (source: National Geographic April, 9, 2009)

Rain Forests

Not all hamburgers come from cows that live on land that was previously rainforest. BUT for every pound of beef raised on land that WAS previously rainforest approximately 660 pounds of precious living matter is destroyed including 20–30 different plant species, more than 100 insect species, and dozens of mammals and reptiles. (source EarthSave.org)

According to a report from Mongabay.com (one of the world's most popular environmental science and conservation news sites), a full 80 percent of the land cleared by Amazon deforestation from 1996-2006 has been used to create cattle pastures. This deforestation in the name of beef has meant the loss of 10 million hectacres in the Brazilian Amazon since 1996. You don't even have to know what a hectacre is to know the situation is severe (btw a hectacre is 10,000 square meters, that still doesn't help, I know).

Michael Pollan, author of *The Omnivore's Dilemma*, was on *Oprah* on Earth Day and he suggested that we try incorporating "meatless Mondays" into our weekly meal plans. I love this idea as it is easy to remember and not hard to do!

If you need more inspiration to go meatless, check out Kris Carr's site www.crazysexylife.com. I am a huge fan!

Waste

My food guilt does not stop with the meat vs. veggie dilemma. I feel rotten about wasting food. My kids (and sometimes I) only eat half of the food on the plate and the other half gets dumped into the disposal. And we're not alone. According to government sources roughly 25% of the food Americans buy goes to waste. That's about one pound of food, per American, per day – thrown in the trash. Jeff Yeagar from TheDailyGreen.com adds, "Sadly we've crossed the line from Land of Plenty, to Land of Waste."

I know there are limited supplies of food on Earth and starving children, and that I shouldn't toss out perfectly good food and yet it still happens. Restaurants and grocery stores are just as bad. Most of the ones I talked to when writing this book throw out perfectly good food each day. I also feel bad when I buy food and then don't eat it before it spoils in the fridge. I eventually reach for it and by then it is way past its expiration date and I end up tossing it. Most people in this world are hungry and yet I still waste perfectly good food... the guilt!

Pre-packaged food and drinks also present a dilemma: I love the convenience of things like snack packs for kids, yet I know that all that packaging ends up in a landfill, and then there is the energy, water and materials to manufacture the packaging in the first place... it's all bad for the Earth! The problem is I am SO LAZY. I am such a deadbeat mom, doing the bare minimum to get by. When it comes to packing their lunches the easy path is to buy prepackaged snacks. The other path is no more difficult, just not what I am in the habit of doing. First of all, I would have to ditch the Power Ranger or Dora lunch box, and get the lunch-box that looks like a tin can with compartments. Then buy in bulk (i.e. large box of snacks). The added bonus is that I would save money as the prepackaged foods cost more. Then in the lunch box compartments, I could just dump the bulk crackers or whatever in the lunch container. Or, I could put in healthy things like orange slices or carrot sticks but my kids don't really go that way. But maybe they would if that were their only option?

Oh, and then there is the need to get one of those Sigg bottles or Klean Kanteens and fill it with water rather than giving them a juice box. Again, not too much of a difference in effort, just a behavioral shift and a needed one as those juice boxes can't be recycled and the sugar in them is not any good for the kids. A tip on the Sigg bottles - only put water in there or they get icky fast. And although one *could* buy the special brush that goes in them that requires scrubbing and I am too lazy to do any more cleaning than necessary. My big issue is that the Sigg bottles are all so darn cute so I have to resist buying more than what is necessary. There is controversy on which is more safe, Sigg or Klean Kanteen, and after much research on my part I found it to be a wash.

Oh, and another thing that makes me cringe is all of the wasted plastic bottles at kids sports events. If I could only remember to bring my kids' Sigg water bottle and encourage other parents to have their kids do the same!

Restaurant Food Guilt...
When I go out to dinner (or when I used to before the financial crisis), I immediately start to stress as I look at the menu... '*Hmmmm should I order the swordfish? I don't know, isn't it overfished or is that the one with the toxic mercury? Shoot... what to do?! What about the cheese in any of these dishes? Does the cheese come from cows injected with RBst and BGH hormone stuff?'*

What I've decided to do about my food choices is split the difference: when I'm out to dinner, I'll enjoy myself and eat up, guilt free! And then, when I'm at home, I'll try to make better choices. It works because I remember: we can't do everything right all the time (at least, I can't. If you can, more power to you!). I'm not saying order filet mignon with farmed salmon on the side. I'm just saying – don't make yourself nuts when you are out to dinner.

Oh, and speaking of better food choices at home you have got to try Strauss organic ice cream even if you think organic food is a crock. It is the BEST ice cream I have ever had. Ironically being the giant chocoholic that I am, I love their vanilla flavor (and mint chip)! Who knew? Although, now that I think about it, dairy comes from cows – ah, the complexity! Well, maybe ice-cream just once a week! And since I eliminated beef, I deserve a little treat now and again. So do you.

Now speaking of treats if you haven't tried Alter Eco chocolate bars, you are missing out on one of life's best pleasures. I like the 73% cacao variety but I know they have less dark ones.

Oh, I forgot to mention a few paragraphs ago that you might like this little handy chart that I put on my site which details which fish is cool to eat. Go to www.showthelove.com/fish to print it out and put it in your wallet.

Drink

It used to be, the only kind of drink guilt I would have is if I drank too much and felt hung-over the next day. I got rid of that by stopping the sauce all together. Now there is this whole bottled water thing. Well, at least I stopped buying expensive bottled water and then lugging it home from the store... what a pain in the ass that used to be.

It turns out that tap water is better for us and the Earth: it is free and comes out of the sink - no lugging or bottle disposal necessary.

It is hard staying up to date on all of this stuff. Just when I think I am 'Miss the-most-green-girl-I-know' I learn that what I thought was right was wrong. Case in point, my water purifier.

Listen to this...

As I mentioned in the beginning of the book the theme of this decade seems to be "what we thought was good is bad." As far as water is concerned, first it was tap. We thought tap water was bad so we drank bottled water. Then we learned that bottled water is bad we went to filtered tap water. So I bought an under-sink reverse osmosis device that cleans my drinking water. Guess what? Apparently reverse osmosis machines use *3-20 times* more water than they produce. They need extra water to flush through the system in order to clean the water that we drink. I am neurotic about not wasting water and I had no idea.

I guess I am going to go back to good old tap water.

Lately, it has become *so* not eco-chic to drink bottled water but hello! Other bottled drinks are doubly bad because those liquids are full of sugars and dyes that are bad for your health and we know that all the plastic bottles are bad for the Earth. So we should actually be speaking out about ALL plastic bottled drinks: not just bottled water.

And speaking of plastic, have you heard of the 'plastic soup?' This gives me so much anxiety. According to scientists there is this giant "plastic soup" of waste floating in the Pacific Ocean that is twice the size of Texas (TWICE THE SIZE OF TEXAS)!!!! This accumulating trash is known as the Great Pacific Garbage Patch. One more reason to drink tap water, not bottled water. (source: National Geographic) If you go to Google and type in 'Great Pacific Garbage Patch' you will see some seriously mind-blowing (and not in a good way) pictures.

Although tap water is perfectly fine to drink I am suspicious of there being too much chlorine in it. Since my reverse osmosis machine is wasteful I have concluded that Brita® pitcher filters might be the way to go from now on, especially since they have partnered with Preserve and are recycling the filters and turning them into things like toothbrushes, cups and cutting boards.

Again, this is a very spoiled problem to have. I should just shut up and be grateful to have any kind of drinking water as we are in the middle of a global water crisis. Here are some hard facts:

- 884 million people lack access to safe water supplies. That's approximately one in eight people.
- Each year 4 million people die from a water-related disease.

- 2.5 billion people lack access to improved sanitation including 1.2 billion people who have no facilities at all.
- Every 15 seconds a child dies from a water-related disease.
- Millions of women and children in countries with poor infrastructure spend several hours a day collecting water from distant, often polluted sources. (source: Water.org and UNICEF)

At any given time, half of the world's hospital beds are occupied by patients suffering from a water-related disease. And I'm worrying about my tap water?! At least I have tap water! But with that blessing comes responsibility. My friend Gary White founded an incredible organization WaterPartners International (Water.org), that is committed to providing safe water and sanitation to people in developing nations.

I love people like that who make things happen rather than people who sit around and complain about them.

Back to the topic of drinking... Apparently we are supposed to buy 'organic' wine, which after looking at that the chart a few pages back, makes total sense. A ton of pesticides are sprayed on grapes, and why would anyone want to drink those? Well, I don't drink because I am boring and get migraine headaches but my husband does and we entertain so I am always buying the stuff. I wonder if he would drink organic wine if I brought it home or if he would just think I was even more nuts?

Gift Giving and Holidays

Gift giving guilt has been around for centuries, I am sure. You give someone a gift, and then they give you an even nicer gift, then you feel guilty for not having gotten them a better gift, or maybe you didn't get them a gift at all, which is even worse... blah blah blah.

Well, perhaps this is where the whole idea of party favors originated from, which is now causing me enormous green guilt. I can't stand party favors and think we should ban them altogether. By eliminating party favors we are eliminating an expense, a hassle, and a toxic bunch of plastic crap that ends up all over our living room floor and then in the garbage (and then in the oceans!).

What I started doing to make myself feel better is giving plants or trees as gifts. Kids actually love having a 'live' something to take care of and grownups love them too.

I read in some magazine recently that the whole eco-gift thing and/or giving a donation to a charity in someone's name is overdone and that it is time to go back to giving traditional gifts. Huh? NO NO NO. I think that the best kinds of gifts are ones that truly give by making a difference and not ones that trash up our planet.

At our house I find what my husband and kids treasure most are gifts from the heart like notes with a commitment to an hour of time together etc. Seriously, I know it sounds "Leave it to Beaverish," but it is true and I have an adorable story that reiterates my point:

Last Easter I was surrounded by hundreds of plastic Easter eggs as I, or rather the Easter Bunny, was stuffing them full of candy and tiny plastic toys. Well, I could only take so much before I started shoving coins into them thinking that money was the lesser evil. In the middle of this stuffing episode I spoke to my girlfriend Ellen who just shook her head when I told her what I was doing. She said that what she did instead of candy, toys or money was to write notes and put those inside the eggs. The notes said things like: *This is Good For One Hour with Mom*, or *This is Good For One Extra Hour on the Computer*, or *You Can Use This to Stay Up 15 Minutes Late Any Night You Wish*. You get the drift. So I wrote notes and shoved some into the remaining eggs.

On Easter morning after the kids had collected the eggs they began opening them and something amazing happened. They didn't care about the candy, money or toys, but the thing they valued most were the handwritten notes (who even knew the Easter Bunny could write and just like mom, no less?). One of my kids was even in tears at one point because he had not yet found an egg with a note that gave him an hour date with mommy (he found one soon afterwards, whew! That Easter Bunny was on the ball!).

A must read for anyone ready to toss out green guilt engendered by holidays and celebrations is the book *Celebrate Green* by mom and daughter team Corey Colwell-Lipson and Lynn Colwell. So many fun ideas in there (and it makes a great hostess gift!).

Electronics Guilt

Because I move a lot I think I feel electronics guilt more intensely than most. I am always purging household stuff that is no longer working and packing up only the things that work. I feel so rotten when I throw something like a broken stereo, lamp, kid's robot, etc. in the garbage. Up until recently, there has been no other alternative. Thank goodness manufacturers have started recycling programs for their products! But even so it is a bit of a hassle to drag the stuff to a drop box somewhere and much easier to toss it in the trash. So I have to work on this one. One thing I am trying now is having a big jar in my utility room where I toss old batteries from toys and then once every couple years I drop them off to the appropriate recycler. But I have a bunch of broken electronics in my garage now and I have to figure out what to do with them instead of dumping them in with regular trash.

We are constantly upgrading our electronic gadgets creating tons of 'e-waste'. GreenPeace International concluded that "The amount of electronic products discarded globally has skyrocketed recently, with 20-50 million tonnes generated every year. If such a huge figure is hard to imagine, think of it like this - if the estimated amount of e-waste generated every year would be put into containers on a train it would go once around the world!"

Do you know what happens when you throw your old electronic gadgets out with the trash? Toxic chemicals, including lead and mercury, contaminate our planet's soils and water supply. Valuable metals, plastic and glass which could have been reused, are wasted.

We can protect the public health AND support businesses that are committed to protecting the environment. How? Just visit www.showthelove.com/ewaste for a list of ways to get rid of your old electronics properly. Some places even let you just fill your own box full of your e-waste and ship it off to them and they pay the shipping! Nice!

Leaving electronics plugged in the wall is another thing I have green guilt over.

According to GreenLivingTips website "The phenomenon of standby, also known as phantom power loads, is responsible for an incredible amount of electricity consumption nationally. Practically every electronic device that you plug into a socket continues to consume electricity *after* you've switched the device off. Examples include phone charges, notebook power adaptors, microwave ovens, game consoles, video and DVD players. You can reduce your electricity bills by as much as 10% - simply by unplugging appliances or switching devices off at the power point they are connected to when not in use."

Short version: reducing electricity use is good for our wallet AND our planet.

So sometimes I try to unplug items but most of the time I don't so I end up feeling bad about the whole thing. I think I am going to have to delegate this responsibility to my ten year old!

Cleaning Products
According to the U.S. Environmental Protection Agency, the air inside the typical home is on average 2-5 times more polluted than the air just outside largely because of household cleaners and pesticides.

Buying the non-toxic cleaner is such a no-brainer: With the green cleaners, your house will be just as clean and germ-free, just less toxic. I feel good about already switching out the toxic cleaning products for healthy ones at my house but I've noticed the cleaning products they use at my kids' schools aren't so eco so now one of my goals is to get those switched out to the non-toxic kind by the start of the next school year.

I am posting on my site some form letters that you can send to your school or office building to request that they start to use non-toxic cleaners. Just go to www.showthelove.com/forms.

Laundry
You know when you go to a hotel and dry off with a towel and a half hour later they have switched out the towel with a fresh one or after one night's sleep they change the bed and wash perfectly

good sheets? I love the 'always freshly washed' feel BUT it is so outweighed by the guilt because I know that unnecessary daily towel and sheet replacements waste so much water and energy. At least I can control that at my house because I am so darn lazy and I wash my towels and sheets as little as possible. In addition, I wash all of my clothes in cold water and try to line dry them. That saves energy and money. All good. By the way, if you want to find sustainable hotel accommodations check out www.wholetravel.com for recommendations.

Dishes

I always get into a fight (well, more like a disagreement) with my husband over the dishes. I think it wastes water when he rinses the dishes and then puts them in the dishwasher. But wait you say, how could you ever be upset with your husband for doing the dishes?! Yes he rocks like that and I am so blessed but he says that the only way they get clean is to rinse them first before putting them in the dishwasher. I think that erases the purpose of the dishwasher and it definitely gives me water waste guilt. These days a lot of dishwasher manufacturers say that pre-wash is unnecessary. Why take the extra effort and waste the extra water? He claims they don't get as clean but I am lazy so I don't care. I go the easy way out on that one.

Eco - Light bulbs

YES they are more expensive, but I do believe they last so much longer so in the end it is the same PLUS two bonuses: One, you don't have to change the bulbs as often and two, they have less of an impact on the environment. If you do decide to switch to eco bulbs, change out the one that you leave on the most, and make sure that you get the kind with soft white light, otherwise you might not end up not liking the fluorescent shade you get. If I were more on it, I would switch out all the bulbs in my house at the same time rather than changing them out one by one as the old ones burn out!

Building

Building a house or remodeling gets into a whole new range of green guilt since now we are now in the "know" and I can't in good conscience build with the toxic products of days of yore. The problem is that building or remodeling is already an over-whelming feat and then to add on top a whole new way of doing things with products that aren't that readily available is hard! I just lived through a remodel and did the best I could, but I do feel guilty for all of the things I couldn't do 'green' because I didn't have the time or resources. But at least I used Low VOC paint (you know, the kind with less volatile organic compounds, aka asphyxiating toxic smelly stuff).

Body Care Products

I am a lotions and potions addict. I have no green guilt here because I buy all of the non-toxic stuff, but I do feel bad because I buy too much of it. Excess is not good for the Earth either. I try to justify it by supporting the good companies that are taking the toxins out of our products. Burt's Bees and Juice Organics are the cheapest and most accessible line without parabens and other junk (as well as recycled packaging). You can get the stuff at any drug store.

You know your skin is your body's largest organ, and when you put most drugstore brands or even fancy pants department store brand lotions on your skin you are getting a good dose of toxins unless they specify no parabens. (Parabens mimic estrogen and are thought to cause an increase tumor growth – yuck!) Anyway, most of us love lotions and potions so why not buy the kinds that are safer for our skin *and* the Earth in the bargain?

However, if you have your favorite wrinkle cream or makeup, don't feel bad if it contains a bunch of toxic ick if it helps make the wrinkles better. Just tell me what it is so I can go buy some myself! (Seriously.)

Oh, and if you have blemishes like I do now and again the best blemish treatment I have ever used, believe it or not, is organic. It is called Juice Beauty - Blemish Clearing Serum. I highly recommend it ☺.

Shampoo, conditioner and deodorant are also items that, if you don't buy wisely, contain parabens. And of course most nail polish contains formaldehyde and toluene (scary). I do my best to make sure to get my toes done with a polish that doesn't harm the Earth or me! I love PeaceKeeper™ Cause-Metics™ as their polish was cited as the safest paint based natural nail polish by the Environmental Working Group, and to top it off they give away their after tax profits to women's health advocacy and human rights groups. Now that is what I am talking about!

Dental Care
I am feeling *so* guilty today as I write this because I was shocked to learn that the retainer that my child wears is made from acrylic plastic, like the kind that smells so bad at the nail salons (no joke). I was actually at the dentist office myself getting a bruxing device (plastic teeth guard) to stop me from grinding my teeth in the night (I know, I need to breathe more) and it is made from the same material! I asked the guy why in the world would I want to shove something that is not made from food grade material in my mouth for 12 hours at a time? Much less into my son's mouth? What am I to do? I just looked it up online and read about how toxic acrylic is. How come no one else is worried about having this in their mouth? I even asked my dentist if it was toxic, and he said they use it for gluing hip joints together. And I said, yes but is it toxic, and he said *again* they use it for gluing hip joints together so I said... so you don't know. He said it is the same stuff they use for acrylic nails (and we all know

how foul that stuff smells) and that he would be interested in finding out what I learned in researching it. I was disturbed by this because we look up to our medical professionals and trust that they are putting safe things in our body. I am probably making something out of nothing, but if your child has a retainer I bet you never even questioned the materials just as we never questioned the plastic baby bottles we were using a few years ago that we found out had BPA in them. I found this on the Made How site about acrylic plastics:

"Acrylic plastics manufacturing involves highly toxic substances...[it] is not easily recycled."

Okay, so now I will have the whole dental community on my case and telling me I don't know what I am talking about (and maybe I don't!) but I am just encouraging us to question things we never thought about before because remember... so much of what we originally thought was safe we now know to be unsafe either for us, our environment, or both. Who knows, maybe retainers are perfectly safe but this is causing me guilt because I know they are not made of non-toxic plastic, and yet I am STILL letting my ten year old sleep with it in his mouth, all night long.

On a bright note, I do use Preserve toothbrushes made from recycled plastic and Tom's toothpaste so at least I'm good on that front...so far!

Paper products
Is it possible to have reverse green guilt? Hmmmm... Some-

times I feel bad for being overly Eco. My Father says that he doesn't like coming to my house because my toilet paper is like wax paper. He thinks I am an Eco-Nazi. So, I do feel bad for being a literal pain in his ass, but what is a girl to do?

He scoffs at my brown paper towels and napkins but I am going to keep buying them though because that is one the easiest green things I can do and I am all about EASY! By the way, the most popular tissue brand that we all know (not mentioning any names) is a blatant environmental offender. Despite public outrage this tissue company is continuing to destroy the ancient Boreal Forest in Canada to make its tissues. The easy way to get them to stop doing that is to stop buying those products! Buy products instead with recycled content.

Disposable Anything
I remember when disposable cameras came out, I thought they were the coolest thing ever and now look how wasteful (thank goodness for digital) those ended up being (not to mention chemical laden, remember that awful smell?)! Although even today with how cheap electronics are we treat cameras and phones almost as if they are disposable, buying new ones every time an upgraded version comes out.

Typical disposables - like plates - have been used for at least the last thirty years. Remember when we went from paper plates to Styrofoam and from Styrofoam to plastic? We thought life was just getting easier and easier.

And then...diapers. Anyone with kids needs therapy after imagining the landfills that their baby's diapers are creating. Thank goodness for companies like Seventh Generation and gDiapers providing more eco-friendly solutions.

Stuff

What a waste of the Earth's resources to be consuming so much junk that is not essential to my everyday life. Jessica Jensen, who founded LowImpactLiving.com says, "**If you want to do ONE THING green, the thing you should do is buy less stuff!**"

Cassie Walker, also from LowImpactLiving, writes, "When you resist the urge to buy something (reducing its demand), you eliminate all of the materials and resources that go into creating the raw materials, manufacturing the item, packaging it, and shipping it. You also cut out the energy and resources you use to go get it and maintain it. And, you keep it out of landfills at the end of its life. Very simple, very easy."

Oh, and the bonus is you save money... how about that!

If you are on a budget the best thing in the whole world to do is to watch www.StoryofStuff.com. You watch that 20 minute cartoon, and you will NEVER want to buy another thing again. Which is exactly what happened to me: I was completely transformed after watching it. Although, BIG WARNING...it increases green guilt momentarily while watching although as soon as you stop buying stuff you will feel better and you end up having less guilt in the end. And besides, it really saves you money. It spoke to me so much that I pledged as my New Year's resolution not to buy anything new all year. Honestly, I resolved to buy NO new stuff for the entire year for myself and my family except for of course food and toiletries. At two weeks into it, I came to some startling conclusions: it wasn't hard, I really enjoyed it and it was totally empowering.

Then came week three...

I broke down and bought organic cotton training pants for my daughter, which could be considered a better alternative to pull-ups (I guess that could be considered "toiletries").

Then I learned some things:

To lay down a hard rule - no purchasing ANYTHING new for an entire year - does not take into account things like needing to buy a Brita pitcher so that I could stop wasting water with my darn reverse osmosis machine and buying things like a brace for my bunion which I really don't want to get secondhand even if I could find a used one.

I also felt like I needed to support the new Green Economy. Our country is a mess financially right now so I feel it is my duty to spend my money at companies that are doing right by the Earth, companies that are using organic or recycled materials, companies that are supporting fair trade practices and companies that are giving back to society.

Therefore, I stopped my program! Now having said that I am still committed to buying secondhand, or borrowing whenever possible (90% of the time) and will not be buying any new conventional products if I can help it but instead if I must buy new, I will support Green Businesses. I realized that is a much wiser commitment to make as I am not just going to do that for a year but for many years to come since sustainability is ingrained in me now.

I look at things through a different lens. Not one of disposable products and limitless resources but one of limited time to keep our resources from disappearing. I want my children to grow up with plenty of trees, fresh air and clean water. Buying new stuff all of the time threatens that. If you don't believe me, I reiterate: just go to StoryofStuff.com. It will change your life (or at least your buying habits).

Clothes

I am a clotheshorse and love to buy new clothes. I have been feeling guilty about buying clothes since as long as I can remember. And for some women it is shoes or handbags in addition to clothes. We know we should be saving our money or spending on something less superficial, and now we have an even greater reason to feel rotten about buying new clothes: We are finally realizing that the Earth has limited resources, and the manufacturing processes involved in making our high fashion statements are not healthy for our planet.

I love the kids' site GreenEdgeKids.com. The folks there tell us what eco-friendly clothing means, and why we should buy it. They write:

"... you first need to understand what happens from the time that a cotton seed is planted to the time that a garment is sold.

The conventional cotton T-shirt sold at your nearby department store has most likely has wreaked havoc on the environment and on people in each step of its long journey around the world to you. The typical story goes like this (it's long, so get a cup of tea and relax while you read on):

First, a farmer plants cotton seeds in some country - China, USA, India, Pakistan, Brazil, Turkey (in order of the world's greatest cotton producers), or perhaps some other country. Most of the time, seeds have been genetically modified, so the cotton plants are resistant to insects. As the plants are growing, plenty of fertilizer is applied. In addition, insecticides are applied to kill troublesome pests, and herbicides are used to kill weeds around the plants. This sounds convenient, but as time passes, even higher doses of chemical pesticides and herbicides are needed on the farm to kill the pests and the weeds. Herbicides are used again right before picking the cotton, to make the picking process easier. Huge quantities of extremely toxic chemicals are used in this type of cotton farming, and guess where these chemicals go as soon as it rains or the farm is irrigated... right into someone's drinking water downstream! Did you know conventional cotton farming accounts for 25% of worldwide insecticide use, according to the Organic Trade Association? The farmer then harvests the cotton and brings it to a gin to separate the cotton fiber from the seeds. From there, it may go to another country for fabric production."

Basically a whole lot of pesticides get dumped on cotton, poisoning our environment. That is a great reason to buy organic cotton products. Bamboo is supposed to be better than cotton because it is a sustainable product but there is still controversy over the way some people are manufacturing the fabric made from bamboo plants.

And by the way, you know what drives crazy? When you see

a truly cute tee-shirt that says something like 'Save the Planet!' and it is made from non-organic cotton. What were they thinking?!

According to Virgina Ginsburg, green living expert who runs GreenBabyGiftsOnline.com,

"A fabric is generally considered eco-friendly (or green) if it possesses the following characteristics:

- Minimum chemical and/or pesticide use on the raw material
- Sustainable planting and farming practices
- A certification of the growers' and manufacturers' eco-friendly operations
- Animal-friendly business practices
- The production of the fabric abides by existing trade practices"

Surprisingly, we are clueless about what makes up the fabrics in which we clothe ourselves! Take rayon. I had no idea what rayon really was or why I should be avoiding it. I just read all about it at GreenAmerica.org and here is what they said:

"Did you know that you can spin trees into cloth? Worldwide, manufacturers make as much cloth from wood pulp as they do from wool.

Rayon is the most common wood-based fabric, but acetate, triacetate, and Tencel® are also made from trees. Unfortunately, turning wood into rayon is wasteful and dirty, because lots of water and chemicals are needed to extract usable fibers from trees. Only about a third of the pulp obtained from a tree will end up in finished rayon thread. The resulting fabrics usually require dry cleaning, which is an environmental concern as well as an added expense and inconvenience.

Much of our rayon comes from developing countries, such as Indonesia, where environmental and labor laws are weak and poorly enforced. There is mounting evidence that rayon clothing manufacturing contributes to significant forest destruction and pollution in other countries."

When it comes to going green changing what we wear can be a painful process. This is different than switching cleaning products or using recycled paper towels. The clothes we buy affect our self-esteem (and we all know that it *shouldn't* but it does). We feel better with a new dress or outfit because society has ingrained in us that shopping equals fun, is a treat, and that we look better with new things blah blah blah. Thank goodness the fashion industry is FINALLY catching on to this save the Earth thing and providing us with more cute eco-choices.

Here is a list of some of my favorite eco-brands and boutiques (A larger list of green clothing companies and their links can be found at www.showthelove.com/fashionsites).

Green With Glamour
Go Green Stay Stylish Boutique for Women, Men, Kids and Home
www.greenwithglamour.com

Shop Envi
Be Green Boutique, Hip, Cool, Clothes for Women
www.shopenvi.com

Nimli
Natural, Organic and Green Lifestyle Clothes
www.nimli.com

Hanna Andersson
Tried and True Staple for All Ages, has a great selection of organic cotton clothes, socks and underwear.
www.hannaandersson.com

Beau Soleil
Stylish Sustainable Women's Clothes
www.shopbeausoleil.com

Fresh and Green
Sustainable Choices for Men, Women, Kids and Home
www.freshandgreen.com

GreenEdge Kids
Designer eco-fashion for children
www.greenedgekids.com

Juno and Jove
Where form and function meet sustainability:
A life emporium for Men, Women and Home
www.junoandjove.com

Perfectly Imperfect
Hip Eco Clothes for Women
www.piorganic.com

Tiny Revolutionary
Organic and Sweat Shop Free Tees for Kids and Adults
www.tinyrevolutionary.com

Beklina
A Green Boutique
www.beklina.com

Atayne
Sports and Performance Wear for Men and Women Made From Recycled Materials
www.atayne.com

Priscilla Woolworth
An eco-friendly general store (actually she sells everything BUT clothes but it's such an awesome site that I had to put it in a list somewhere! Check her out!)
www.priscillawoolworth.com

Still my big problem is quantity. How many tee-shirts or pairs of jeans do I really need? At least I am now broke in this struggling economy so I am not able to buy as much stuff!

Junk Mail and Magazines
Going to my mailbox is not the fun that it used to be when as a little girl I would go and find a letter from Grandma. No more! Now our mailboxes are filled with catalogs that I cannot help but see as trees that have died in vain. Thank goodness for Mail-Stopper (www.greendimes.com) where you can sign up to have them remove you from all of those junk mail lists. Still there are the sneaky marketers that manage to get to me. One particular

company that we are all familiar with (but I don't want to single them out as many are doing the same) mails out more than 395 million catalogs a year - more than 1 million a day! Now that translates to a lot of trees being cut down and a lot of junk mail in landfills...oh and the ink required to print catalogs: not good for the environment either.

So if I want to be a good world citizen, I can either *(a)* stop shopping at stores that send out catalogs or *(b)* sign up for MailStopper or *(c)* both *(a)* and *(b)*. BTW, I love that MailStopper plants five trees for each person who signs up! They also have gift cards – how cool is that?

Over time, I believe we are going to be relieved of this excess paper as you would not believe what is happening to the physical mailbox - you know the one that sits outside of your house. It is going to disappear! At least if ZumBox has anything to do with it.

What is ZumBox? It takes a minute to get your head around it because it is different than email but imagine no more trees being cut down for paper mail, no more postal trucks and planes polluting the environment to deliver junk mail, and no more worrying about putting your mail on vacation hold. ZumBox is assigning online mailboxes for every address in America, so all of your bills and correspondence will arrive there instead. Way cool! (www.zumbox.com)

Even with that new technology I still have magazine guilt because I can't stop buying them even though I know they are rotten for the planet. Can you believe that one giant magazine publisher (again, trying to be discreet) that publishes various Green Issues *refuses to use recycled paper to make its magazines*?! Magazine production contributes extensively to deforestation... the United States magazine market alone results in more than 35 million trees being cut down each year and enormous amounts of water and energy. BTW, that publisher I referred to a few sentences ago was named one of America's Toxic 10 Corporate Polluters, by Green America, a nonprofit membership organization dedicated to harnessing the economic power of consumers, investors and businesses to promote social justice and environmental sustainability.

So bottom line: If we want to do our part we need to try to resist the urge to buy magazines! And if you are like me and *must* read them get a subscription for the online version and/or share with a friend, or read them at the doctor's office or in line at the check-out counter (then it is free!). Or check out e-magazines like *Cocoecomag* (www.cocoecomag.com) or *Antler* magazine (www.antlermag.com).

In case you are wondering... YES, the same goes for books too! Better to borrow them from library... except for THIS BOOK OF COURSE... (ka-ching!)... but really, this book is printed using ethical publishing and a percentage of revenues from the sales of this book go to fund environmental charities so don't feel bad for buying this one!

Holiday Cards
Unlike junk mail, holiday cards are one of the best things to find in your mailbox! But when it comes to sending them out myself I have guilt regardless of the green issue. I feel guilty if I don't do them, guilty if they are late, guilty if I don't write a note in them blah blah blah. Oh, and when is it okay to throw your friends'

picture card in the trash after you get it? Some people hold on to them for years until they have whole boxes of past holiday cards filling their garages. I throw them away immediately (sorry friends).

I just switched last year to a 'virtual' card which is when you send an email greeting vs. snail mail. I did it through SmileBox. com and it was a giant hit. People loved them and I benefited hugely because it is so darn easy to push a button and have all of your holiday greetings sent out in an instant.... no addressing, licking, stamping and schlepping to post office. Just voila! And it's free! And in my entire life of sending cards, let's say for the last 20 years, I have never received such a great response. My card played music, had multiple photos and was interactive. Immediately people emailed back and then I got to write back to them! That does not happen with a paper card. I mean nobody even writes a personal note any more... so in the end the e-card turned out to be a real winner.

Literal Green Guilt
Seasonal plants: Poinsettias, for example. You buy them, decorate your house and then let them wither and throw them away. You can't really plant them outside because they are tropical (unless of course you live in the tropics). If you're a better person than I am you keep them year after year until your entire house is one big poinsettia farm, blooming year round, out of season 11 months out of the year.

For the most part though, potted plants are better than cut flowers. Did you know that most cut flowers have all kinds of toxic pesticides on them? They are poisoning the people that are collecting them in the fields and greenhouses and inevitably harming the end buyer/recipient as well. Of all the flowers, roses have the most pesticides sprayed on them. So I feel extra bad when I don't buy organic roses but instead pay less for toxic ones. I try to order from organicbouquet.com especially when sending bouquets to friends and family.

(A secret: I even feel guilty for killing weeds, so I have real issues, but who is to say what is a weed and what is not?)

Trash and Recycling
I live in what must be one of the most eco-conscious towns in the country. Our trash service is literally called Green Waste Co. They recycle everything! What really gets me is when I go to another part of the country and I realize that not everyone else is required to recycle the way we are in Northern California. Like when I visit my parents in Texas and I want to dispose of a glass bottle or can or newspaper, I have to dump it with all of the regular trash because their town doesn't offer recycling along with their regular trash pick-up service. Then I feel awful as I toss everything into the same bag that I know will end up as a huge landfill. Yikes.

I'm curious – if you're reading this book and live somewhere other than the West Coast, what does your town do for recycling or not do that you'd like them to do? Maybe getting a group of friends together to kindly but firmly lobby your local council on a single community recycling initiative would be a cool group thing to do together!

"Be the change you wish to see in the world."
-Mahatma Gandhi

Hot and Cold

Sometimes when I'm in an office, store or hotel building that has the air conditioning or heat blasting I get so annoyed because that kind of extreme indoor temperature control is just blowing money AND carbon emissions out the window. I feel like somehow it is my responsibility to write a letter to the owner or manager and set them straight. Of course I haven't yet done that so I feel bad about that (but now there are form letters on my site so we can click and send a pointed note to any business that could consider a few environmental changes – www.showthelove.com/forms).

At my house I try my best to keep the thermostat set only a few degrees above or below what I can stand depending on the season. It makes a difference.

As far as the hot water heater is concerned I have no problem keeping that thing turned down to the recommended 120 degrees as it helps prevent scalding and saves money.

Speaking of hot, we love to make fires all winter long but recently someone REALLY burst my bubble about this and now I feel bad any time my husband throws a log on the fire. Here in Northern California, we have No Burn days (also known 'spare the air' days) and if THEY (meaning: anyone!) catch you burning a fire on those days the police give you a violation and you have to go to some kind of school program (think traffic school) to teach you how bad burning fires is for the environment. Turns out that it *is* super bad. The smoke from wood fires is a much bigger carcinogen than cigarette smoke and when millions of people burn fires on same night it really pollutes the air. So my solution is to buy those Java Logs or EnviroLogs. We are still not allowed to burn them on the No Burn days but at least on the other days I am okay with sitting by the fire.

FYI here is some information on Java Logs:

- Made from all renewable materials
- Non toxic
- NOT petroleum based
- Doesn't cause ozone depletion
- Produces 87% less carbon monoxide than wood
- Will burn up to three hours

If you have a natural gas fireplace they are even better for the environment because they don't produce any debris but I am not ready to give up the crackle and pop.

(I just realized that I might be creating additional green guilt for you...but hopefully by the end of the book I will have you in a better place than when you started.)

Bedding etc.

I feel rotten letting my kids sleep on mattresses filled with toxic flame retardants (PBDEs) in their flame retardant pajamas and laying their heads on the flame retardant pillows (okay, well, they only use the toxic pillows when they are on the couch watching TV). This PBDE stuff is nasty. It is short for some industrial toxic chemicals used for more than 30 years to retard flames in consumer electronic plastics, furniture, and mattresses. According to the Washington Toxics Coalition:

"At very low levels PBDEs impair memory, learning, and behavior in laboratory animals. They also affect thyroid hormones and other bodily functions. Most at risk are developing fetuses, infants, and young children. There is strong scientific evidence that levels of PBDEs are rising rapidly in the environment and in human bodies, particularly in North America where the use of PBDEs is the highest.

- Recent studies by Environmental Working Group and Northwest Environment Watch show that women in Washington State and the United States have levels of PBDEs in their breast milk that are much higher than the levels found in European women.

- Studies in wildlife have shown that PBDE levels are rising at alarming rates, doubling every one to five years."

Needless to say all of this makes me totally neurotic as I can't at this point afford to go and replace my PBDE laden mattresses, pillows, rain coats and outdoor furniture etc. Although I did buy my toddler an organic mattress for her big girl bed.

I know by now you are thinking I should up the meds or see a therapist. This book is *supposed* to be therapy. Yikes... But we're going to get there together in the end so hang tight and keep reading.

Appliances
As far as appliances go, there is a Sub Zero fridge, once prized by homeowners, in the home we bought. When I look at it I see a giant energy sucker conspiring to ruin the Earth. I can't grab a carton of milk out of it without feeling guilty. It really makes a difference to switch your appliances out to ones with the Energy Star® rating. I try to tell my husband this and he tells me it is worse for the Earth to trash a perfectly good refrigerator.

True, but the EPA still encourages us to change over to a new one. "A 20-year old refrigerator or freezer can consume two to four times more energy annually than a new model, and, as a result, can significantly increase your electric bill. Older refrigerators or freezers put a great strain on local power grids, especially during peak hours. By replacing your old refrigerator or freezer with a newer model, particularly one that has earned the government's ENERGY STAR® label, you can conserve energy and save upwards of $50/year. If your old refrigerator is a secondary unit located in a basement or garage, you can save over $100/year on electricity charges by removing it and not replacing it.

Some utilities will actually pay you to get rid of your old refrigerator or freezer through bounty programs or rebate programs."

Nice, so maybe that is my answer.

Plumbing
To Flush or Not to Flush, that is the question...

Is it just me or do you sometimes feel guilty flushing the toilet? And of course I am talking tinkle here nothing else! If you don't flush then the toilet gets icky faster and God forbid you have a guest drop by and they see an unflushed potty. But if you do flush for every single little tinkle then you are wasting water. Unless you have one of those way cool dual flush toilets. I love those! You push one button for tinkle, and one for um, the other... Nice.

Now if I could only get my husband to remember to not let the water run while he is brushing his teeth and to make sure the kids don't let the toilets run. At least I just bought a shower timer so my soon to be teenager doesn't spend an hour in the shower!

Plastic bags

Just looking at plastic bags can make me want to put them over my head. How many plastic bags do we need? None, really. It's easy to cut the ones we use for grocery shopping down to zero – all we have to do is remember to bring our own bags to the supermarket. As for snack bags, I now try to use these cellulose ones that are bio-degradable (available at greenhome.com). They are clear plastic looking bags (no zip lock feature) that you can close with a twisty and they work great for most everything.

Candles

I can't burn a conventional candle without guilt because I know they are made from petroleum products and pollute our indoor air. If you take a piece of white paper and hold it above a burning candle you will see what I mean. The paper will turn black (don't burn the paper!). So I am trying to switch all of my candles out for ones made of soy. They at first seem more expensive but they burn so much longer than conventional candles so they are actually less expensive in the end.

According to Simran Sethi at Huffington Post:

"Most candles are made from paraffin wax, which is derived from crude oil. Demand for these products plays into our reliance on fossil fuels. When burned, paraffin wax emits carbon. Yep, carbon emissions in your own home! A group of Israeli environmentalists even used candle-happy Hanukkah to highlight the carbon issue. The safety or potential toxicity of smells released as gases from fragranced candles is unknown. Anyone who got a headache from too much French Vanilla in 1996 can attest to the sketchiness of these potions. Older candles, the sort you've had in the Emergency Kit for twelve years, might have lead in their wicks. These babies are banned in many parts of the world, including the U.S. in recent years, but they slip into the market and wreak unhealthy havoc on indoor air quality."

Travel
So anyone who has been paying any attention at all over the last five years knows that driving and flying around disperses tons of carbon emissions into the atmosphere. I feel bad anytime I drive somewhere but most especially when I am at the gas station pumping toxic liquid into my ever so chic puke green minivan. I finally traded in my SUV as the minivan - although not a hybrid - gets better gas mileage than an SUV.

"It is the confession, not the priest, that gives us absolution."
-Oscar Wilde

Now What?
As you might have figured out, I could ramble on forever about environmental things that bring me down. But what bothers me will be different than what bothers you. So to complete step three of our five- step program get out your pen and paper and write your own list of things that give you green guilt. This should be a cathartic process. By writing things down we somehow see them as more manageable. When you have finished with that, circle the top three things that cause you the most stress. Seriously, go ahead and get your pen and paper out now!

- **Write a list of things that cause you green guilt and/ or eco anxiety.**

- **Prioritize the list by circling the top three stressors.**

STEP 4

"The world is a dangerous place, not because of those who do evil, but because of those who look on and do nothing."
-Albert Einstein

Anxiety and guilt are toxic emotions that can be released through the *breath,* put at bay with *acknowledgment,* replaced with positive *affirmations,* identified through *writing* and lastly redirected by taking *action.* That brings us to our fourth step of the five-step program.

a c t

Pick *one* thing to do that is 'green' that you aren't already doing, and start doing that one thing today. Do that one thing WELL. You'll feel better doing one thing well than eight things poorly.

This part of the book was the hardest for me. Not because it is hard to take action (although it *is*) but because I did a lot of research and at first I was not convinced that my actions really mattered. I have come full circle though as I went from believing the small things we do matter to believing that nothing we do matters and I am now back to the beginning believing that *'yes, we can'* make a difference! This Margaret Mead quote illustrates my belief beautifully:

"Never doubt that a small group of thoughtful committed people can change the world: indeed it's the only thing that ever has!"
-Margaret Meade

Here is how my mental journey came 360.

My plan initially called for taking baby steps. I was thinking that we would take a look at the items we circled on our list, pick the one that was bothering us the most and then do something proactive to eliminate it off of our list. I thought, realistically, we are not going to change ourselves or the world overnight. We just want to stop feeling rotten over the whole thing and this would surely help us feel like at least we were doing something.

Then I went to a Thomas Friedman lecture, a Jeffery Sachs lecture and a Lester Brown lecture, each of which blew my mind. I learned what a seriously dire situation our world is in as far as global warming is concerned. I began thinking that all of the things on my list of green guilt really didn't make that much of a difference as far as really turning this ship around.

Jeffrey Sachs, the author of *The End of Poverty, Economic Possibilities of Our Time* and Director of the Millennium Project, reminded me that the lack of access to clean water is one of the biggest obstacles for getting people out of poverty and that with global warming this problem is exacerbated. Malaria, dengue and cholera are all on the rise with the increase in global temperature. (source: Science Daily)

Lester Brown, population expert and founder of the environmental think tanks Worldwatch Institute and Earth Policy Institute, highlighted the issue of our growing population, and how it is taxing the planet. He says, "between now and 2050, three billion people will join the six billion-plus that already live on this planet. How will we possibly feed all of them?" Brown, who has been called by the *Washington Post*, "one of the world's most influential thinkers" definitely got ME thinking (and scared)! In his book, *Plan B 2.0, Rescuing a Planet Under Stress*, Brown addresses issues such as falling water tables and rising global temperatures that imminently threaten our world's food supply.

According to world-renowned author and journalist, Thomas Friedman, none of this easy stuff is really going to make a difference (although he still encourages doing it). He notes that while we can change our light bulbs, it might be vastly more effective to change our leaders; and that we need to reward companies and lawmakers for progress in promoting clean energy. In his latest book, *Hot, Flat and Crowded*, he calls for "Code Green" – a green revolution. He quotes Mao Tse-Tung, *"Revolution is not a dinner party, not an essay, nor a painting, nor a piece of embroidery; it cannot be advanced softly, gradually, carefully, considerately, respectfully, politely, plainly and modestly."* Revolutions don't happen overnight or without effort or sacrifice.

Right now, using trendy words like *green* and cool catch-phrases like *eco-chic*, we are comforting ourselves: making small gestural changes that make us feel like we are making a difference.

A green revolution on the other hand, will not be easy. It is not something we just check off on a list of green guilt items. We will need to work hard to change current mind set, and demand of ourselves and our countries that we get off oil and coal. We need to revolt and demand clean energy solutions from our government and private companies.

"The ecological crisis is doing what no other crisis in history has ever done - challenging us to a realization of a new humanity."
-Jean Houston

So... I was beginning to feel that most everything I felt guilty about, I could just stop fretting over. I thought: when you break it down, we don't really need to do small acts of lifestyle changes like going organic (although it is certainly healthier for us and the Earth) what we really need to do is stand up and be counted. To make our voices heard by writing our congress people and organizing rallies and educating ourselves on this most critical issue.

As Rob Watson, environmental consultant, says in Friedman's book, "People do not seem to realize that it is not like we are on the *Titanic* and we have to avoid hitting the iceberg. *We have already hit the iceberg* and the water is rushing in down below. But some people just don't want to leave the dance floor; others don't want to give up on the buffet. But if we don't make the hard choices, nature will make them for us. Right now, the acute scale of this problem remains confined largely to the expert scientific community, but soon enough it will be blindingly obvious to everyone."

That is pretty serious stuff, and again I began feeling overwhelmed. But then I remembered something from the oh so wise Lao-Tzu, "The journey of a thousand miles begins with a single step."

That reminded me of what I initially believed: that if we don't start making these small steps then who will? And that together our small steps will get bigger and cover greater distances. We need folks to do small things and folks to do big things. We need to attack this from every angle possible.

Bono had a great *tweet* on Twitter that illustrates this point: "It is too often that we confusing 'planning' with 'doing'. Great movements begin with foolish and clumsy first steps. Begin."

One person can't do it all (unless you are the genius who invents a cheap, renewable clean energy) but we are not in this alone. As I mentioned earlier we are more than 6 billion strong, with another 3 billion coming in the next 40 years (yikes!).

If we all come together we can find solutions to this crisis. Surely we can mobilize to get our leaders on board to pay more attention to this issue.

So I return to my original sentiment:

Start small and within reason and think of how you can eliminate something off of your list. By doing something proactively to help remove even *one* of those items on your list you will start to feel more in control and less guilty. Choose something easy and doable. Eventually after it becomes second nature to you then pick another one from your list and so on.

"If you are not a part of the solution, you are part of the problem."
-Anonymous

Make It Happen
Okay, so you are not ready to lobby Washington for clean fuel or a gas tax but you want to do little things to get rid of some guilt.

In case you need guidance on how to take action I have made a list of things you can try, broken down from easy to hard. Doing even ONE of these things will help diminish green guilt.

Some of these are things we can do to keep from trashing the planet. And some are things we can do to keep this excess of CO_2

from killing us all... nice! Oh and if you don't want to read this now, it is on my site at showthelove.com/act .

Easy & inexpensive ways to eliminate GREEN GUILT

Replace 3-5 frequently used incandescent light bulbs with compact fluorescent bulbs (CFLs) - or just turn out the darn lights when you walk out of a room!

Run your washer and dishwasher with full loads- gotcha, I can do this one.

Adjust your heater thermostat down two degrees in winter (wear a sweater) and up two degrees in summer (use a fan) – easy peasy.

Use 100% post-consumer recycled paper in your printer and copier – done!

Take shorter showers; turn off the water when soaping up and shampooing and while brushing your teeth – okay, will do if I must...

Buy minimally packaged goods – no problem!

Don't idle your car; turn off the ignition if you'll be waiting more than 30 seconds (unless you're in traffic...) - this one is so cool because I use to think that it wasted more gas to turn off and on but no. Just shut it down while you wait for those kids to climb in.

Recycle your paper, aluminum, plastic, and glass trash – and recycle batteries, paints, and broken electronics- I am so good like this.

Unplug electronics that are not in use (including your computers and printers) and unplug surge protectors at night – maybe I should put up post-it notes for this one... I remember to unplug most things but not those darn surge protectors.

Unplug chargers when the charge is complete – This one is easy because they get so hot left in that it worries me.

No more "paper or plastic" bring your own reusable bag to the store – Come on, with all of the cute bags out there, we all should be able to do this, my challenge is to remember them even when I am just running in for ONE thing but inevitably end up buying more like twenty!

Eat less meat – done! Easy for me, but probably harder for some. Just read that book *Skinny Bitch* and you won't eat meat again!

Lower your hot water tank temperature to 120 degrees – This is so key and only takes 30 seconds to do.

Don't flush medicine down the toilet, find a local drop-off facility (call your local city hall for locations) OMG, I just learned why this is a bad thing to do...did you know they are finding birth control meds and antidepressants in fish and our drinking water?!?!

Have a "no shoes" policy at your front door – apparently this reduces the need to vacuum as much which is a good thing for saving energy and saving my back, but I have never been able to implement this one but I will try to do so!

Recycle your clothes – shop for clothing at thrift stores and donate outgrown clothing to charity (or swap with friends)- This one is a piece of cake, no need to dump more chemicals on cotton plants so we can wear something new! I love to shop at Goodwill for myself and my kids.

Don't wash your car at home; take it to the carwash – OMG I had no idea about this one... apparently the run-off water full of chemicals/gasoline etc goes into the ocean when we wash it at home, but at a carwash they have federal guidelines requiring them to catch the water and dispose of it properly! Wow, who knew?? Well I can beat that, I don't wash my car at all! Nice!

Take the cargo carrier off the roof – I mean if you have one of these ugly things on your car it is an eyesore and a gas guzzler, take it off for goodness sakes, unless you're going camping or skiing...

Take extra junk out of your trunk – yikes! This one is targeted at me I know! I am so so messy and my car is full of junk!

Drive the speed limit – I know, this one is hard to keep to but doing so saves gas and it is a good idea especially since 3000 people die in car crashes a DAY worldwide.

Water your yard in the morning, preferably pre-dawn – Doing this minimizes evaporation and plants won't stay wet all night long and develop root rot... also, snails like to come out at night and who wants to see drowned snails first thing in the morning when looking out at their garden? Yuck.

Use "green" cleaning products – A cinch now that they are mainstream.

Wash your laundry in cold water – I love this one because it is SO EASY and makes a big difference.

Pay bills online; go paperless when you can – better for your bookkeeping too!

Stop most junk mail - register at www.dmachoice.org or go to mailstopper.tonic.com or BOTH. Love it!

Freecycle (www.freecycle.org): Give and get stuff for free in your own town – keep good stuff out of landfills.

Use the library – Only buy a book if you want it around the rest of your life- I just started doing this and love it.

Adjust sprinklers to eliminate runoff onto pavement – I am in charge of this at my house because we have a huge water bill, it was a pain in the ass but worth it.

A little more effort... (and/or a little more money)

Keep your automobile tires properly inflated; check them on a monthly basis – okay this one is not so easy for me and probably won't happen...but you never know!

Install a low-flow showerhead - I put on a showerhead that takes out the chlorine to keep my hair from turning green and my skin from getting too dry. It also slows the flow a little!

Clean or replace air conditioner and furnace filters as recommended – oh yeah, I better do that as I don't like that lint stuff blowing all over my house.

Buy products and produce locally – I totally lucked out on this one because a half of a mile from my house is an ORGANIC farm stand! Some places though this can be a challenge, but that's where the internet comes in super handy, check out www.localharvest.org for a place near you

Use public transit, carpool, or ride your bike once a week – hmmm this one is so hard, but so necessary. Okay, maybe I can pick up another kid and drive them to school!? I live by Stanford University and they have a big sign that says, Got Glaciers? And then a few feet later another sign says, Are You Driving Alone?... the guilt!

Plant a deciduous tree and native, drought-resistant plantings – I love this one. I feel like nature girl when I plant a tree! Of course it helps that I live in the middle of nowhere with lots of places to plant one. If you live in the city then just get online to treepeople.org and have a tree planted in your name or the name of a friend as a gift.

Insulate your water heater and water pipes – This is so out of my league.. Can anyone say handyman? When in doubt: consult an expert.

Caulk and weather strip your doors and windows – Again, I am thinking handyman here but I can see how both this one and the water heater one would really save on heating bills and CO_2 emissions so I guess I better find Bob the Builder.

Use a push mower and rake instead of gas mower and blower – You might scoff at the thought of a push mower, but have you ever breathed in any of those fumes from the gas mowers and blowers. YUCK!!! Apparently they are SUPER DUPER TOXIC... like way worse than exhaust from our cars because our cars have filters for the fumes and these don't! Also: great way to combine exercise and a nice looking lawn. (side note, same goes for snow mobiles... nasty, resist the urge).

Buy organic food, organic clothing, organic bath and body products – This involves shopping and no handyman necessary, so totally up my alley. Organic may cost a little more but we are worth it! (ditto the Earth!)

Line-dry your clothes - especially sheets and towels – okay, more power to you if you can do this one. For me, it is a no brainer to line dry because the dryer shrinks and ruins things faster than I don't know what, but I don't like to line dry my sheets and towels because they don't feel as soft...at least I am not using fabric softener anymore.

Start using a reusable water bottle; Sigg or Klean Kanteen – Piece of cake.

Contact your local utility company about alternative energy options – that is a good idea, I am going to do this one! We definitely have that out here on the west coast but every energy company in America should be offering alternative energy options. The only way that is going to happen is if enough people demand it.

Make sure your car is properly aligned and tuned-up- Ugh a trip to Jiffy Lube, okay I guess I can do this, and my car needs an oil change anyway! Properly aligned tires save on gas and, as a result, gas emissions.

Install a programmable thermostat- I hear this is a great way to save on heating bills and to reduce carbon emissions. I just need a lesson on how to work mine.

Repair leaks and running toilets-I think we all are on this one already-no one likes a leaky faucet or running toilet.

Install outdoor motion sensors—don't leave the porch light on- Aha! This is a good idea. I need to do this. I guess I had better get that handyman (btw most people can sort these without handy men or women... I am just easily overwhelmed and my husband works 100 hours a week so he doesn't have time!).

Use a laptop instead of a desktop computer- Easy for me because that is already what I use but apparently this will save a ton of energy.

Use low-VOC (Volatile Organic Compound) paint, especially in the bedroom – Okay, I have to say you are a total MORON if you don't do this one. Who wants to breath in toxic fumes all of the time when there is now non toxic, no smell paint available? The trick is educating the painters or any other construction folks you have helping you with your project. The only way to ensure you get the right stuff is to go to buy it yourself. Trust me, don't delegate this. I got screwed on this by two different contractors, even though I spelled it out for them!

Drink Tap...Install a water filter on your faucet if necessary for drinking or use Brita pitcher – As you read earlier I love Brita! easy easy easy...

More effort and more money, but more reward ....

Install low-flow toilets and faucets – In my dreams I will have the dual flush toilets. Not happening anytime soon unless I build new house, but you go right ahead and make it happen!

Invest in green business, green energy - HUGE... this one is so important. I just joined a green bank for my business that invests in green energy. It is called New Resource Bank. I also want to learn more about investing in alternative energy as that is so critical right now. This might be the first thing I do (as soon as I finish this book I am going to Google it, and learn what to do!).

Plant a vegetable garden; even better, replace your lawn with a vegetable garden- I planted a veggie garden last year and LOVE IT! Problem is you have to weed it, which I suck at. And I have dreams of tearing out my lawn and putting low water plants and pebbles in its place. My husband demands the kids have a place to kick the soccer ball so for now he is winning, but maybe I can at least rip up half the lawn?! Or convince him to use public grounds?

Replace old appliances with Energy Star® appliances- I just did this with my old washing machine and am dying to do it with my refrigerator because the fridge is the single largest energy drain appliance in the house.

Make sure your walls and ceilings are insulated, and install double pane windows- My house is old and poorly insulated- not good. Can't afford to switch out windows now, but maybe it will reduce heating bills in long run?

If you live in a sunny climate, install a solar thermal system to help provide your hot water and a solar photovoltaic system to generate electricity- I hear you don't have to pay anything up front anymore for these things and you only have to pay monthly the same as what you would be paying in electric bills (but you wouldn't have those anymore). Check out www.globalsolarcenter.com and they will tell you if it is worth it or not to switch to solar (i.e. if your monthly bill will be cheaper using solar power!).

Install a gray-water system and re-use water from the bath and washing machine for your landscaping- wow this sounds cool!! I wish I had one of these. I do use our bathwater to water my houseplants though!

"What I try to tell people is don't sweat the small stuff," says Chip Giller, founder of *Grist*, a well known environmental news site. "An individual can have more impact if they focus on bigger purchasing decisions." Buying a hybrid car or a water-and-energy-saving washer and dryer has more impact than worrying about paper or plastic, he says.

According to GreenAmerica.org:

The Five Things You Should <u>Always</u> Buy Green Are:

1. Paint: Look for LOW, or ideally no-VOC paint.
2. Paper: Look for paper products with a high post-consumer recycled content.
3. Light bulbs: Look for compact fluorescents.
4. Appliances: Look for Energy Star label appliances.

And...

Ten Things You Should <u>Never</u> Buy Again Are:

1. Styrofoam Cups
2. Paper Towels
3. Bleached Coffee Filters
4. Teak and Mahogany
5. Chemical Pesticides and Herbicides
6. Conventional Household Cleaners
7. Toys made with PVC Plastic
8. Plastic Forks and Spoons
9. Farm Raised Salmon
10. Rayon

Initiating a Green Revolution:
If checking things off the aforementioned list is so yesterday to you or just not your cup of tea then think about joining one or

more of the many great organizations that are working hard to increase awareness and prevent further climate change. I am going to get involved at this level because my green guilt is so severe that I think working with one of these organizations is my only cure!

By the way, even if you have no interest in contributing at this level it is actually healthy to read about the organizations I am mentioning below because you will see that the revolution has indeed started. People are making great progress, and it is inspiring. But they can't do it without us! So if you have it in you, try getting involved!

GreenForAll.org is a national organization dedicated to building an inclusive green economy strong enough to lift people out of poverty. By advocating for local, state and federal commitment to job creation, job training, and entrepreneurial opportunities in the emerging green economy – especially for people from disadvantaged communities – Green For All fights both poverty and pollution at the same time. (I love that!)

Green For All believes a shift to a clean, green economy can improve the health and well-being of low-income people, who suffer disproportionately from cancer, asthma and other respiratory ailments in our current pollution-based economy. Such a shift can also create and expand entrepreneurial, wealth-building opportunities for American workers who need new avenues of economic advance. (Yes!)

In other words: they believe that the national effort to curb global warming and oil dependence can simultaneously create well-paid green-collar jobs, safer streets and healthier communities. Super cool, huh?

In order to make that happen they do the following:

- Link activists and advocates, organizations, policy makers, practitioners, and business, labor, and community leaders together in dialogue to advance the vision of a green economy that benefits all Americans;

- Lift public awareness on the potential of green-collar jobs to transform the economy, curb global warming, and build pathways out of poverty;

- Leverage best green practices and policy into model programs and legislation that can be adopted at the national, state or local level;

- Provide technical assistance to mayors and community groups to implement local green-collar job initiatives; and

- Build an on-line community of practice to convene thought-leaders and share leading program models, technical documents and templates.

EcoMomAlliance.org is a global organization inspiring and empowering thousands of women, through education and community action, to help reduce the climate crisis and create and environmentally, socially and economically sustainable future.

Here is what they say on their site:

- We empower women to become advocates and change agents within their communities.

- We provide both in person and web based outreach education, connection and education.

- We create strategic partnerships to bring forth targeted campaigns that promote social change, a green economy, and environmental stewardship.

- We support policy that helps propel financial, ecological and social health, particularly as it relates to women.

- We work with companies to develop sustainable business standards and practices.

GreenSchoolAlliance.org is an alliance of K to12 public, private and independent schools uniting to take action on climate change and the environment. The GSA was created by schools, from schools and is working with and through schools worldwide to promote energy conservation and environmental awareness and responsibility. The GSA is comprised of students, parents, school heads and administrators, business officials, facility managers, trustees and school boards, teachers, and staff all working together to ensure a safe and healthy environment for future generations through the implementation of sustainable, energy-smart solutions today.

Change.org serves as a central platform informing and empowering movements for social change around the most important issues of our time such as social and environmental problems ranging from health care and education to global warming and economic inequality. For each of these issues, whether local or global in scope, there are millions of people who care passionately about working for change but lack the information and opportunities necessary to translate their interest into effective action.

1Sky.org was created in 2007 to focus the power of millions of concerned Americans on a single goal: bold federal action by 2010 that can reverse global warming. The 1Sky Solutions are grounded in scientific necessity – they are the bottom line of what's needed to dramatically reduce carbon emissions while maximizing energy efficiency, renewable energy and breakthrough technologies. They also represent significant economic promise. By pivoting to a clean energy economy, we can relieve our dependence on foreign oil, unlock the potential of sustainable industry and usher in a new era of prosperity and green jobs.

"At this defining moment in the climate change crisis, 1Sky unites scores of groups and individuals in a collaborative campaign with a single purpose: shifting federal policy in the United States towards the prosperity of a sustainable, low-carbon economy." (Now that is what I am talking about!) I love their new campaign:

"Across the country, Climate Precinct Captains (CPCs) are stepping up in their communities, playing a critical role in building one of the strongest and fastest-growing grassroots movements in history.

As a CPC, you can organize your local precinct through events and actions, working to turn your Members of Congress into climate leaders."

Not ready to start a group yet? Join an existing group to start taking action in your community. There's no time to wait!

CoopAmerica.org is a not-for-profit membership organization founded in 1982. (They went by the name "Co-op America" until January 1, 2009.) Their mission is to harness economic power – the strength of consumers, investors, businesses, and the marketplace – to create a socially just and environmentally sustainable society. They work for a world where all people have enough, where all communities are healthy and safe, and where the bounty of the Earth is preserved for all the generations to come.

What Makes Green America Unique

- They focus on economic strategies-economic action to solve social and environmental problems.

- They mobilize people in their economic roles - as consumers, investors, workers, and business leaders.
- They empower people to take personal *and* collective action.
- They work on issues of social justice *and* environmental responsibility. We see these issues as completely linked in the quest for a sustainable world. It's what we mean when we say "green."
- They work to stop abusive practices *and* to create healthy, just and sustainable practices.

Carrotmob.org is a method of activism that leverages consumer power to make the most socially-responsible business practices also the most profitable choices. Businesses compete with one another to see who can do the most good, and then a big mob of consumers buys products in order to reward whichever business made the strongest commitment to improve the world. It's the opposite of a boycott.

1 Block Off the Grid (1bog.org) is a nationwide effort to create local community based buying clubs for products that reduce our energy footprint and promote energy independence. By banding people together and negotiating on their behalf 1BOG takes the fear out of buying new green technologies and significantly increases the adoption rate of these technologies while helping *everyone* in the process obtain a better price.

1BOG started as a consumer-based initiative in San Francisco and quickly grew to the largest group-purchasing program for green products in the country. By organizing a large group, they drive down pricing by negotiating with service providers.

EnvironmentAmerica.org is a federation of state-based, citizen-funded environmental advocacy organizations. Their professional staff in 27 states and Washington, D.C., combines independent research, practical ideas and tough-minded advocacy to overcome the opposition of powerful special interests and win real results for the environment. Environment America draws on more than 30 years of success in tackling environmental problems.

StopGlobalWarming.org is Laurie David's pioneering movement. On her site, you can join the virtual march on Washington, learn how to petition your mayor and learn other ways to get involved to make sure your voice is heard. Laurie has a telling quote on her website:

"We shall require a substantially new manner of thinking if mankind is to survive."
– Albert Einstein

There are hundreds of other organizations rallying to turn this planet around. Be a part of the movement! We will be making history!

Recap

So that was a lot of information I just dumped on you. Let's remember the big ideas here:

- **Although it is not immediately obvious one person's small actions *do* make a difference. (Look at the election process in the U.S. for goodness sakes, every vote counts!)**

- **Pick one thing off your list of green guilt and take some action to remove it from the list. (If you feel bad you haven't switched out that light bulb that you leave on all night, switch it out already!) You will feel** accomplished, worthy and the Earth will thank you!

- Take as small or big of steps as your life permits but know that by taking any step at all that you have begun the journey of making this planet better for your children.

- Just in case you are feeling guilty AND lazy or you don't feel like doing anything, but you do want the problem to go away, then maybe a donation to Green-4All.org will do the trick. You can always fund the people that are making it happen!

3 Easiest Things to Do That Have the Biggest Impact

1. Elect Good Leaders
2. Buy Less Stuff
3. Eat Less Meat

And...remember The Three R's!

1. Reduce
2. Reuse
3. Recycle

STEP 5

"The universe is change; our life is what our thoughts make it."
-Marcus Aurelius

Whew! We are on the home stretch! It is almost time to tie it all together. So ideally you are *breathing, acknowledging, affirming, writing* and *acting.* Look how far you have come! You are making things happen and deserve a big pat on the back! Which brings us to the final step in our five-step program!

<u>praise</u>

Make a mental note to be proud of yourself, your family, your friends, your town, your company, your country *whenever* a step is taken in the right direction.

You can't repeat this step often enough. In fact, take a moment and praise yourself right now for taking the time to pick up this book taking a look at your environmental impact.

"The thought manifests as the word. The word manifests as the deed. The deed develops into habit. And the habit hardens into character. So watch the thought and its way with care. And let it spring from love, born out of concern for all beings."
-Buddha

Someone once told me that the problem with being a grown-up is that no one ever sits down and tells you that you are doing a good job, that you are on track, or any of that stuff that kids get in school. Kids get measured on how well they are doing academically, socially and physically. Parents say *great job* when the kids do something good, or *what a beautiful picture*, or *way to go*, but no one ever pats us (or at least me!) on the back with any positive feedback. It is true. So it is up to *us* to tell ourselves that we are doing a great job. We should be proud of ourselves for waking up and seeing that what we have been taught to do and believe for the last 30 years in regards to the environment is wrong.

Self talk and praise goes back again to the affirmations we were working on in Step 3. I found this passage from DailyPostiveAffirmation.com very relevant:

"A person's will is so powerful that it must be nurtured by constant repetition of positive self-talk. It serves as the engine for the human body to move and move faster. The lack of it would deprive you the chance to move forward from the first level of personal growth. Always remember that any form of development would require a clear affirmation of your goal and vision."

As we complete small tasks off of our green guilt lists we need to genuinely congratulate ourselves. Being aware of our positive self-talk is crucial, as is remembering to tell ourselves that we are proud of ourselves for being a part of the solution.

"The greatest revolution in our generation is the discovery that human beings, by changing the inner attitudes of their minds, can change the outer aspects of their lives."
-William James

Praise is a pretty straightforward and seemingly easy thing to check off on our program list yet it is just as critical component as any of the more time consuming tasks and the one you are most likely to forget to do.

So to reiterate:

- **After doing even the smallest 'green' task, take a deep breath and smile upon yourself. Be proud that you are part of the solution.**

- **If you want to, repeat an affirmation as well. "I am helping make the world a better place" or "I am proud of myself" or "I do a great job."**

- **When you see others doing something good for the Earth: compliment them!**

CONCLUSION

"This is a series of great opportunities disguised as insoluble problems."
-John Gardner

spark

Congratulations! You have just finished the Official 'Bag Green Guilt' Five-Step program to eradicate feelings of green guilt and eco-anxiety, and replace them with inspiration and empowerment. But don't put the book down yet. Let me leave you with some feel good thoughts to get you on your way!

The cool thing about green guilt is that we can do something about it. We just need to breathe, get our minds clear, and focus on tangible things we can do to improve our life and the life of our planet.

We have limited time to sort this whole thing out. We don't have the luxury of sitting around feeling guilty and anxious with our heads in the sand. We can't let those emotions paralyze us. We are better than that. And our children definitely are, and they deserve every chance at a bright and breathable future. Let's keep these emotions from drowning us, instead, let them spark a fire in our guts.

A spark that fills us with the passion to stand up and seize back our life and our planet. One that motivates us to get involved rather than to get depressed. One that gives our life meaning and purpose outside of being a parent, brother, sister, son or daughter, husband or wife. One that gives us a feeling of pride, rather than guilt, knowing that we are doing all that is in our power to make it all better.

If you are not ready to lead the Green Revolution you can always begin with small steps at home.

Starting small is better than not starting at all.

Some of us might think that becoming more *green* means more work on our part, more money and more stress but it is actually the opposite. Once we are able to shift our behavior patterns that were ingrained in us for at least the first half of our lives then we can easily incorporate anything *eco* into our routine and save money while doing it. It doesn't have to be done overnight, or at all for that matter, but if you took the time to read this book, then you are so ready to make it happen! If not you, who?

"If I am not for myself, who will be for me? If I am not for others, what am I? And if not now, when?"
-Rabbi Hillel

The best thing we can do for our planet is elect good leaders and use our voice. It is not just at the Presidential level that this matters. We need to get in front of lawmakers and companies and petition, buy or boycott and rally for real change.

You will find your unique way of how you want to contribute.

"Your life's work should be found at the intersection of your greatest passion and the world's greatest need."
-Henri Nouwen.

I think that is part of the secret. Finding out what it is about you that you can offer as part of the overall solution. What are you good at that you would enjoy offering to humanity?

Just incorporating green things in our lives is not the complete answer. We need to speak up and be counted. The powers that be need to know that we are concerned about these issues and that we are willing to undergo short term sacrifices for long term preservation.

Use your voice, speak up, be heard. My guess is this will eliminate your guilt or hopefully diminish it! I know I feel better after writing this book and speaking my mind!

We live in a time of tremendous opportunity to make a positive impact. We are the cause and answer to the world's problems. We just have to decide in our mind to focus on being the solution and make it so. We can choose to have anxiety, guilt and inaction or we can choose hope, inner strength and action. I am choosing to act. It feels much better than sitting around feeling like crap. Try it. You might like it, and you'll not only help yourself, but you'll help the Earth in the process.

"The difference between a successful person and others is not a lack of strength, not a lack of knowledge, but rather a lack in will."
-Vince Lombardi

Are you still feeling stressed about all this? Well, I will remind you: it is never the things you worry about that get you in the end.

But in the end, even the smallest difference is a difference.

Breathe.

Peace and love,

Jen

Copyright 2009

Don't you just love this photo? I liked it so much that I blew it up and put it on the wall in my office. My friend Stephanie took this picture of her then 14 year old daughter Emma. Try for a minute to jump up and cross your legs like that and look totally Zen while you are at it. Emma is our future. She is a green leader amongst her peers and is a girl with a heart of gold. This photo gives me inspiration and assurance that yes, with future leaders like Emma, the world IS becoming a better place.

Still Have Guilt???
Then visit www.showthelove.com/baggreenguilt and write on our Wall of Guilt. It is very therapeutic!

If we do not change our direction, then we are most likely to end up where we are headed.
-Chinese Proverb

And check out this amazing comment by Jacob Riis, Photographer and Journalist:

"When nothing seems to help, I go and look at a stone cutter hammering away at his rock perhaps a hundred times without as much as a crack showing in it. Yet at the hundred and first blow it will split in two, and I know that it was not that blow that did it - but all that had gone before."

See? We can do it one step at a time and it *will* make a difference.

Okay, I am going to stop writing now. Thank you so much for reading my ramblings. I am very grateful. Now let's go and make things happen! (Okay, maybe I will need a little chocolate first.)

THE END

Note: As discussed in the book, information on this topic changes quickly. To stay current on this subject, visit www.showthelove.com daily!

ABOUT THE AUTHOR

Jen Pleasants is an eco-anxiety ridden mother of three. After more than ten years in marketing and advertising she went on to found the original 'Show the Love,' a jewelry, clothing and body products company, in 2003, dedicated to raising money and awareness for charity. Over time, Jen decided to turn her manufacturing/design business into a media business and use her growing knowledge and interest in everything green/eco to help make the world a better place. She is the publisher of showtheLOVE.com, a site that combines green save the world things with fashion, celebrity and trends. Jen lives with her husband and children in Northern California.

"Don't let eco-anxiety ruin your life:
use it to save your life *and* the planet."

Notes:

Breinigsville, PA USA
14 October 2009
225863BV00001B/9/P